Asian Cooking

BARNES &NOBLE BOOKS
NEW YORK

Contents

Asia's Rich Variety
Typical ingredients

Asia is a continent of many different peoples and cultures, and its cooking offers an equally enormous diversity. Even so, there are some characteristics that apply throughout: Asian cuisine is fresh, colorful, and always aromatic, it uses a large number of herbs and spices, and its main cooking methods are stir-frying, steaming, and deep-frying. In Asia, these are ancient traditions, but to us they seem exciting and new. Why should that be? Is it because the list of ingredients reads like a guide to good nutrition—plenty of vegetables and grains, with low-fat fish and little red meat? Hardly! The main reason for the huge success of Asian dishes, from spring rolls to vegetable curries, is that they taste fabulous. The fine ingredients are cooked in ways that preserve their flavor, aroma, and vitamins, often in a wok, which even in the West is winning over more and more keen amateur cooks. This is because stir-frying is quick, and the finished dishes look wonderful, as the short cooking times make sure they keep their color and texture. The key to success is to use fresh ingredients, most of which can now be bought from a neighborhood store. And because Asian cooking is continuing to boom, many exotic herbs, spices, and other ingredients are now being sold in good supermarkets.

1

COCONUTS (left) are used in Asian cooking in a wide variety of ways. The flesh is combined with water and other ingredients to make coconut milk, which is available in cans. With its delicate aroma and creamy consistency, it adds a milder note to hot dishes, such as curries.

1 LIMES have seedless flesh that is very juicy, highly aromatic, and quite sharp. Both the juice and the rind are used.

2 CURRY PASTES are used mainly in Thailand, where they come in yellow, green, and red varieties. All of these are very hot.

3 LEMONGRASS is a reed-like herb. Normally only the bulb is used, although sometimes the stalks are added to give extra aroma, but they are removed before serving. The plant has a lemony aroma and a slightly sharp flavor.

4 PAPAYA, sometimes known as papaw or pawpaw, is a tropical fruit. It is beautifully soft and juicy, and has an aroma somewhere between an apricot and a melon. It is ripe when the skin turns yellowish and soft to the touch.

5 BAMBOO SHOOTS are the young shoots of bamboo grass, and are cut like asparagus. They need to be cooked in order to remove toxins and bitterness and are widely available canned.

6 TAMARIND PODS contain a slightly sour pulp which is used as a spice to add flavor and acidity to many dishes.

7 BOK CHOY is also known as spoon cabbage. It is very similar in appearance and use to many Western greens, but has a much milder flavor than cabbage. It can be eaten either raw or steamed.

7

GINGER ROOT, whether freshly grated or chopped, gives many Far Eastern dishes their typical flavor. For a less intense spicy flavor, you can use galangal, which also belongs to the ginger family.

NOODLES in Asian cooking are made from wheat, buckwheat, or coarse whole-wheat flour. Special varieties are transparent glass noodles (made from mung bean starch), and rice noodles, which are produced from thin rice flour dough.

PALM SUGAR is obtained from the fruits of a special type of palm. The fruit juice is boiled down to a thick, syrupy consistency, then dried. It is used mainly in Thailand as a seasoning. You can substitute brown or raw sugar if it is unavailable.

SAMBAL OELEK is a ready-prepared, Indonesian paste made from red chiles, salt, and vinegar or tamarind juice. It is used both for cooking and as a spicy accompaniment or dipping sauce.

SESAME OIL is pressed out of roasted sesame seeds. Because of its nutty flavor it is used as a seasoning, rather than as a cooking oil.

SOY SAUCE is the universal seasoning of almost all Asian cuisine. The dark, salty sauces from China and Japan are especially popular.

6

Step by Step
The most important techniques

There is no need to buy any special equipment for cooking Asian dishes—standard pots and pans will do. However, if you like Asian cooking and want to do it frequently, a few traditional pieces of equipment will prove useful. First and foremost is the Chinese wok, which has now become very popular in the West. It does not take long to learn how to cook with a wok, so long as you follow a few simple rules. The most common use for the wok is stir-frying. For this technique, the most important rule is that you should not start cooking until all the ingredients have been washed and chopped or sliced, as necessary, and the various sauces and seasonings are ready at hand. Another popular method of cooking in China and Japan is steaming. The ingredients are cooked slowly in hot steam, and so retain their nutrients and aroma. The wok is also ideal for deep-frying. The great advantage here is its shape, which narrows as it becomes deeper. This means that relatively little oil is needed and that, as the ingredients are added one by one, they are rarely completely submerged in it.

Steaming and stir-frying—the secrets of success

1 Set the clean wok on the stove and start by placing a suitable wooden rack or trivet in the base.

2 Fill the wok about one-third full of water. Place the lid on top and bring the water to a boil over medium heat.

3 Place the ingredients in a bamboo basket, place it on the rack or trivet, cover with the lid, and cook until tender.

1 Pour the oil into a preheated wok and swirl it around. Start by cooking onions, garlic, or other similar ingredients, stirring and tossing constantly.

2 Next add the vegetables. These should all be evenly chopped or sliced to the same size. Fibrous vegetables should be added first.

3 Turn and stir the vegetables constantly, so that they never lie on the hot surface for long. When cooked, push them to the side of the wok.

How to prepare fresh spring rolls

1 Dip the sheets of rice paper into warm water, then spread them out on a clean dishtowel. After about 2 minutes they will have softened.

2 Cover the lower third of the rice paper with a lettuce leaf (not too crisp or it will break when rolled), and the remaining filling ingredients.

3 Roll up the filling in the rice paper, at the same time folding the edges inward. As you roll, add extra ingredients, packing them in tightly.

4 Shortly before you finish rolling, you can complete the "package" by adding some halved scallions, fresh chives, or garlic chives.

How to make chile flowers

1 Using a sharp knife, halve the chiles from the tip until just before the base of the stalk. Carefully scrape out the seeds and remove the membranes.

2 Cut the flesh into thin strips, still attached at the stalk end. Place in ice water for about 20 minutes, until they open up into flowers.

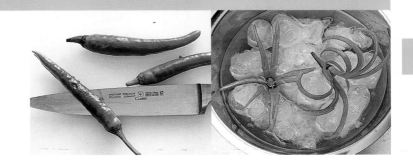

How to prepare sushi rice

1 Place ⅓ cup sushi rice in a strainer and rinse under cold running water until the water runs clear.

2 Place the rice in a pan with scant ½ cup water, bring just to a boil, then cover, and simmer gently for 15 minutes.

3 Remove the lid, then leave to swell for 10 minutes more. Meanwhile warm two pinches each of salt and sugar in one tablespoon rice vinegar.

4 Transfer the rice to a bowl, sprinkle with the marinade, and mix together with chopsticks. This recipe is sufficient for about 12 rolls.

Soups & Snacks

Noodle Soup
with Spinach and Shrimp

What makes this appetizing soup such a winner
is that it is not only delicious, but also a real delight to the eye

Ingredients

1 bunch of **scallions**

7 ounces fresh **leaf spinach**

salt

2 ounces Chinese **egg noodles**

1 cup **shiitake mushrooms**

2 cups peeled cooked **shrimp**

1 tablespoon **oil**

1 teaspoon grated fresh

ginger root

3¼ cups **vegetable stock**

1 tablespoon **soy sauce · pepper**

Preparation
SERVES 2

1 Rinse the scallions, then trim off, and discard the green ends. Cut two of the white parts lengthwise almost halfway along into narrow strips, and place in ice water for about 1 hour, until they open out into flowers. Cut the remaining white parts into thin strips about 2 inches long.

2 Rinse the spinach, then place in a pan with a little lightly salted, boiling water, and cook until just wilted. Strain and let drain.

3 Cook the noodles in lightly salted, boiling water according to the package instructions, until they are tender, but still firm to the bite. Strain and let drain.

4 Wipe the shiitake mushrooms and slice thinly. Rinse the shrimp under cold running water and pat dry with paper towels.

5 Heat the oil in a preheated wok or pan, add the scallions, and stir-fry briefly. Add the ginger and stir-fry for a few minutes. Pour in the vegetable stock and add the mushrooms, then simmer for about 4 minutes. Season with soy sauce and pepper. Finally, add the shrimp and heat through.

6 Place the noodles and spinach in two small bowls and pour over the hot soup dividing the vegetables and other ingredients equally among them. Serve garnished with the scallion flowers.

Shrimp Soup
with Hot Chile

Nothing could be finer than this Thai soup, in which fresh lime leaves
mingle with the hot taste of chiles against a background of spicy shrimp

Ingredients

10½ cups unpeeled, raw **shrimp**

1½ cups **shiitake mushrooms**

1-inch piece of fresh **ginger root**

1-inch piece of **galangal**

2 **lemongrass stalks**

3 **kaffir lime leaves**

4 small **red Thai chiles**

2 tablespoons **oil**

½ teaspoon **black peppercorns**

2–3 tablespoons **Thai fish sauce**

3 tablespoons **lime juice**

salt

Preparation
SERVES 4

1 Wash the shrimp, then twist off, and reserve the heads. Peel off and reserve the shells. Using the point of a sharp knife, remove the dark vein that runs along the back of each shrimp. Rinse the shrimp under cold running water, pat dry with paper towels, and set aside in a cool place.

2 Wipe the shiitake mushrooms, then cut off, and reserve the stems. Peel the ginger and galangal and slice thinly. Rinse and finely chop the lemongrass. Wash the lime leaves. Halve the chiles lengthwise, seed, and rinse the flesh.

3 Heat the oil in a preheated wok or pan. Add the reserved shrimp heads and shells and cook, stirring constantly, until they turn pink. Add the mushroom stems, ginger, galingal, lemongrass, 2 lime leaves, and 2 chiles. Pour in 4 cups water, add the peppercorns, and simmer for 30 minutes.

4 Slice the mushroom caps. Remove the central rib from the remaining lime leaf, roll up the two halves of the leaf, and cut them into thin strips. Thinly slice remaining chiles.

5 Strain the shrimp stock, return it to the wok or pan, and bring back to a boil. Add the mushrooms and cook for 5 minutes. Add the shrimp to the stock and simmer briefly over low heat until they have changed color. Season the soup to taste with fish sauce, lime juice, and salt, then sprinkle with the remaining lime leaf and strips of chile. Serve hot, garnished with flowers or cilantro leaves if you like.

Broccoli Soup
with Shiitake Mushrooms

Preparation
SERVES 2

1 Rinse the broccoli, then separate into small flowerets. Peel and dice the thick stems. Place the bean sprouts in a strainer, pour over hot water to blanch lightly, and let drain. Wipe the shiitake mushrooms, and slice thinly. Peel and finely chop the garlic.

2 Heat the oil in a pan, add the mushrooms and garlic, and cook for about 3 minutes, stirring constantly. Add the broccoli, Chinese stock or vegetable stock, and scant ½ cup water. Cover and cook for about 10 minutes over medium heat, until the broccoli is just tender but still retains some crispness.

3 Add the bean sprouts and season the soup with soy sauce, sesame oil, salt, and pepper.

4 Rinse the cilantro or parsley and shake dry, pull the leaves off the stalks, and sprinkle over the soup.

Ingredients

9 ounces **broccoli**

1 cup **bean sprouts**

1½ cups **shiitake mushrooms**

1 **garlic clove**

2 tablespoons **oil**

1 cup **Chinese stock**

(or 2¼ cups vegetable stock)

1–2 tablespoons **light soy sauce**

1 teaspoon **sesame oil**

salt · pepper

3 fresh **cilantro sprigs** (or parsley)

Ingredients

5½ ounces **salmon fillet**

4 cups **vegetable stock**

2¾ ounces **buckwheat noodles**

1 teaspoon **bonito flakes**

1 tablespoon **light soy sauce**

salt

cayenne pepper

1 tablespoon **lemon juice**

garlic chives

(with flowers if you like)

Noodle Soup
with Slices of Salmon

Preparation
SERVES 2

1 Rinse the salmon fillet, pat dry with paper towels, and cut into thin slices. Heat the stock in a pan, and add the buckwheat noodles and cook for about 3 minutes.

2 Place the salmon slices in the stock, and simmer gently over low heat for about 3 minutes more, until the noodles are tender, but still firm to the bite. Stir in the bonito flakes.

3 Season the soup with soy sauce, salt, cayenne pepper, and lemon juice. While it is still hot, divide among two small bowls or soup plates and garnish with the garlic chives. If you like, a few fine strips of presoaked nori seaweed may also be added. Jumbo shrimp can be used in this soup instead of the slices of salmon, and for those who like a hotter flavor, the mixture can include a chile sliced into thin rings.

Miso Soup
with Bean Curd

Sheer seduction: This classic Japanese soup—made here with bean curd and fine noodles—is the ideal start to a successful Asian meal

Ingredients

For the dashi stock:

6 x 6 inch piece of

kombu seaweed

3 tablespoons **bonito flakes**

For the soup:

2 teaspoons **wakame**

3 tablespoons **miso paste**

salt · **pepper**

3½ ounces firm **bean curd**

2 **scallions**

7 ounces **Japanese wheat noodles**

1 fresh red **chile**

1¾ cups **bean sprouts**

1 tablespoon **oil**

1 teaspoon **sesame seeds**

2 tablespoons **cilantro leaves**

Preparation
SERVES 4

1 Gently wipe the kombu with a cloth, but do not rinse. Place it in a pan, add 3½ cups water, and gradually bring to a boil over medium heat. As soon as the water begins to bubble, remove the kombu, then bring the water back to a boil.

2 Add the bonito flakes and bring to a boil again, then remove the pan from the heat. Let stand for about 1 minute, until the flakes have sunk to the base of the pan, then strain the stock through a cheesecloth-lined strainer into a clean pan.

3 Soak the wakame in cold water. Heat the dashi stock and stir in the miso paste until it has completely dissolved. Season the soup with salt and pepper.

4 Rinse the bean curd, pat dry, and cut into cubes. Add to the soup, and simmer gently for 4–5 minutes. Rinse the scallions, chop, and add to the soup.

5 Place the noodles in hot water, bring to a boil, and cook according to the package instructions, then drain, and immediately rinse in cold water.

6 Halve the chile lengthwise, seed, rinse the flesh, and cut into strips. Place the bean sprouts in a strainer, pour over hot water to blanch lightly, and let drain. Heat the oil in a preheated wok or skillet, stir-fry the bean sprouts and chile, then add the sesame seeds and stir-fry briefly. Divide the noodles, bean sprouts, and wakame among four small bowls, pour over the hot soup, and serve garnished with cilantro leaves.

Chicken Soup
with Rice and Curry

A concentrated dose of strength from the Far East: Chicken and rice
in a finely seasoned stock are good for both the stomach and the soul

Ingredients

9 ounces skinless, boneless

chicken breast portions

1 teaspoon **light soy sauce**

2 tablespoons **apple juice**

2½ cups **chicken stock**

¼ cup **basmati rice**

salt · pepper

curry powder

Preparation
SERVES 2

1 Rinse the chicken and pat dry, then cut it into small cubes.
Combine the soy sauce and apple juice in a shallow dish, add the
chicken, and marinate for about 30 minutes.

2 Bring the stock to a boil in a pan. Meanwhile, place the rice in a
strainer and rinse well under cold running water until the water
runs clear. Add the rice to the boiling stock and cook over low
heat for 15 minutes.

3 Add the chicken with its marinade to the stock and bring to a
boil. Simmer over low heat until the chicken is tender and cooked
through. If necessary, add a little extra water.

4 Season the chicken soup to taste with salt, pepper, and curry
powder. Pour the soup into small bowls or soup plates and if you
like, serve garnished with fresh cilantro leaves.

**This chicken soup can be turned into
a light stew by adding some colorful
diced vegetables. For a spicier flavor,
season with a little wasabi, the green
horseradish paste from Japan.**

Spring Rolls
with Sweet and Sour Sauce

Delicious flavors galore: In this recipe, the popular
little parcels are not deep-fried in oil, but gently cooked over steam

Ingredients

3 tablespoons **dried mushrooms**

12–16 frozen **spring roll wrappers**

5 ounces **pork tenderloin**

1 tablespoon **all-purpose flour**

1 **carrot**

1⅓ cups canned **bamboo shoots**

2 sprigs each **basil** and **mint**

3 tablespoons **oil**

3 tablespoons **soy sauce**

5 tablespoons **vegetable stock**

1 teaspoon **cornstarch**

1 bunch of fresh **chives**

For the sweet and sour sauce:

2 **tomatoes** · 2 **garlic cloves**

⅔ cup **meat stock**

1 tablespoon **light soy sauce**

4 tablespoons **sugar**

2 tablespoons **light vinegar**

salt · **pepper**

Preparation
SERVES 4

1 First, make the sweet and sour sauce. Place the tomatoes in a
bowl, pour in boiling water to cover, and let stand for 2 minutes.
Drain, skin, halve, and core them, then finely dice the flesh. Peel
and finely chop the garlic. Put the tomatoes and garlic in a pan
with the stock, soy sauce, sugar, and vinegar and place over
low heat. Season with salt and pepper, heat gently for about
8 minutes, then remove from the heat, and let cool.

2 Meanwhile, soak the dried mushrooms in lukewarm water for
about 2 hours, then drain, and slice thinly.

3 Spread out the spring roll wrappers to thaw. Thinly slice the pork,
cut into ½-inch pieces, and toss in the flour. Peel the carrot, drain
the bamboo shoots, and cut both into thin strips. Rinse the herb
sprigs, shake dry, then pull off the leaves, and chop coarsely.

4 Heat 2 tablespoons of the oil in a pan. Add the bamboo shoots
and carrot and stir-fry briefly. Pour in the soy sauce and cook for
3 minutes. Heat the remaining oil in another pan and stir-fry the
pork until browned. Reserve 1 tablespoon of the stock and add
the remainder to the pork. Stir in the vegetables and herbs.
Combine the cornstarch with the reserved stock, mix to a smooth
paste, and stir into the pork mixture. Spread the mixture along
the center of the wrappers, fold in the sides, roll up the
wrappers, and tie up the rolls with chive stalks.

5 Place the spring rolls in a steaming basket over a wok or pan
partially filled with boiling water, cover, and cook for about
8 minutes. Serve hot with the cooled sweet and sour sauce.

Rice Paper Rolls
with a Vegetable Filling

Preparation
SERVES 4

1 Place the rice paper between damp dishtowels to soften. Peel the carrots, then cut lengthwise into thin strips. Separate the lettuce into leaves, wash, and spin or shake dry. Halve the red bell pepper lengthwise, then seed, and rinse it. Cut the flesh into thin strips.

2 Combine the white wine vinegar and oil in a small bowl and season to taste with salt and pepper. Mix thoroughly to make a sauce.

3 Lay 1 or 2 lettuce leaves on each sheet of rice paper. Cover with a few strips of carrot and red bell pepper and sprinkle with the sauce. Fold in the sides and carefully roll up the sheets of rice paper. Cut each roll diagonally across the middle and arrange the halved rolls on plates, standing on their straight ends.

4 Wash the garlic chives and shake dry, then insert the stalks, in small bunches, into the rice paper rolls.

Ingredients

4 sheets of **rice paper**

2 **carrots**

1 small **lettuce**

1 **red bell pepper**

1 tablespoon **white wine vinegar**

3 tablespoons **oil**

salt · pepper

1 bunch of **garlic chives**

(with flowers if you like)

Ingredients

4 cups **oil**, for deep-frying

3½ ounces small **shrimp crackers**

For the dip:

1 tablespoon **tamarind pulp**

¼ teaspoon **shrimp paste**

3 **apples** · 1 ripe **mango**

1 **orange** · ½ fresh **pineapple**

1 small **cucumber**

4 **scallions**

1 teaspoon **sambal oelek**

3 tablespoons **sweet soy sauce**

scant 1 cup **palm sugar** (or raw sugar)

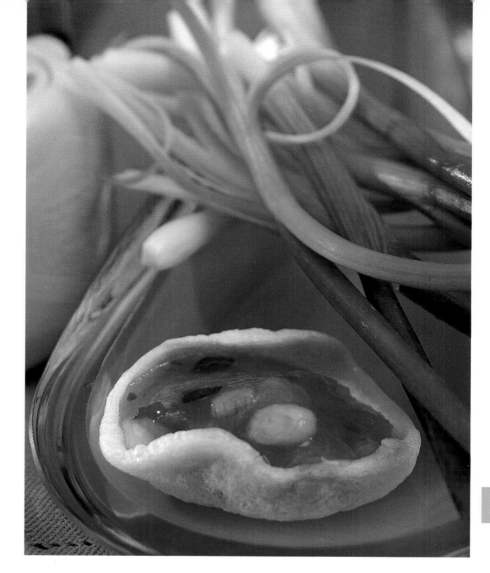

Shrimp Crackers
with a Sweet and Sour Dip

Preparation
SERVES 4

1 Heat the oil in a pan until it bubbles when a chopstick is held in it. Drop in the shrimp crackers, one at a time, and deep-fry for a few seconds, until puffed up and crisp, but not brown. Remove with a slotted spoon and drain well on paper towels.

2 Combine the tamarind pulp and shrimp paste with ⅔ cup hot water. Peel, core, and dice the apples. Peel, pit, and dice the mango. Peel the orange and cut the flesh into

pieces. Cut off the top of the pineapple, peel, halve, remove the core, and dice the flesh finely. Rinse the cucumber, halve lengthwise, scoop out the seeds, and dice finely. Rinse the scallions and cut into rings.

3 Push the tamarind pulp mixture through a strainer. Combine the tamarind liquid with the sambal oelek, soy sauce, and sugar. Mix the diced fruit and vegetables into the dip and serve with the shrimp crackers.

Deep-fried Wontons
with Rice Balls

A **double** surprise: Inside the crispy wrappers there's juicy chicken
with corn, and the rice balls have **spicy** ground beef at the center

Ingredients

For the rice balls:

generous ½ cup **short grain rice**

1 **onion** · 2 **garlic cloves**

1 **carrot** · 1¼ cups **mushrooms**

2 tablespoons **oil**

14 ounces **ground beef**

1 tablespoon **soy sauce**

2 tablespoons **sesame oil**

1 tablespoon **sesame seeds** · 1 **egg**

curry powder · **salt** · **pepper**

For the wontons:

2 tablespoons **rice vinegar**

1 tablespoon **honey**

3 tablespoons **soy sauce**

½ teaspoon **ground cinnamon**

2 **garlic cloves**

14 ounces **skinless, boneless**

chicken breast portions

⅔ cup canned **corn** · 1 **scallion**

8 **spring roll wrappers** · 4 cups **oil**

Preparation

SERVES 4

1 For the rice balls, simmer the rice gently in a covered pan containing 2¼ cups water for about 25 minutes, until the water has been absorbed. Then spread out on a dish and let cool.

2 Peel and finely dice the onion, garlic, and carrot. Wipe and finely dice the mushrooms. Heat the oil in a preheated wok and stir-fry the vegetables for a few minutes, until softened, then let cool. Mix with the beef, soy sauce, sesame oil, and sesame seeds. Separate the egg, reserve the yolk, and stir the white into the stuffing, then season with curry powder, salt, and pepper. Using damp hands, roll the mixture into little balls, and coat with rice. Cover and set aside in a cool place.

3 For the wontons, combine the vinegar, honey, soy sauce, and cinnamon. Peel and chop the garlic, add to the mixture, and season with salt and pepper. Rinse the chicken, pat dry, and cut into small cubes. Place in the marinade and set aside for 30 minutes.

4 Drain the corn. Rinse and finely dice the scallion. Add the corn and scallion to the chicken. Cut each spring roll wrapper into 4 squares of equal size. Place 1 tablespoonful of the filling in the middle of each, brush the edges of the wrapper with beaten egg yolk, and fold the corners toward the center like an envelope. Press the edges down firmly.

5 Pour water into a large pan to a depth of ¾ inch, place the rice balls in a steaming basket, cover, and steam for about 15 minutes.

6 Deep-fry the wontons in hot oil until golden brown, remove, and drain on paper towels.

Temaki Sushi
with Vegetables

Simply irresistible: Crunchy vegetables and hot wasabi
paste give these elegant sushi cones that certain something

Ingredients

1¼ cups **sushi rice**

2½ tablespoons **rice vinegar**

1 teaspoon **sugar** · **salt**

2 **eggs** · 1 teaspoon **butter**

1 **cucumber**

1 **daikon**

a few **frisée leaves**

10 sheets **nori seaweed**

2 teaspoons **wasabi**

scant ½ cup **soy sauce**

Preparation
SERVES 4

1 Rinse the rice in a strainer until the water runs clear. Pour generous 1½ cups water into a pan, add the rice, and bring to a boil. Lower the heat, cover, and simmer for about 15 minutes. Remove the lid, and leave the rice to swell for 10 minutes more. Meanwhile, place the rice vinegar, sugar, and 1 teaspoon salt in a small pan and heat gently. Transfer the rice to a bowl, sprinkle with the marinade, and mix with chopsticks.

2 Whisk the eggs with a pinch of salt. Melt the butter in a skillet, add the eggs, and cook until they form a thin omelet. Slide the omelet out of the skillet and cut into thin strips.

3 Wash and peel the cucumber and daikon, and cut lengthwise into thin sticks. Wash the frisée leaves, shake dry, and tear into small pieces. Cut each sheet of nori seaweed into 4 equal pieces .

4 Place some rice, strips of omelet, cucumber sticks, daikon sticks, a few pieces of frisée, and a very small amount of wasabi on each piece of nori. Roll up each piece of seaweed into a cone. Serve the temaki in decorative bamboo dishes if you like, with the soy sauce for dipping.

You can fill temaki however you like, depending on your mood and what is in the refrigerator. Cooked, smoked, or raw fish (salmon or tuna) will go well, as will cooked shrimp, or almost any vegetable.

Nigiri
with Mussels

Preparation

MAKES 10 NIGIRI

1 If the mussels are from a can or jar, drain thoroughly, rinse, and drain again.

2 Wash the parsley, and shake dry. Reserve 10 leaves for the garnish, and finely chop the remainder.

3 With damp hands, roll the cooked sushi rice into 10 small balls of equal size, then flatten them slightly on the base with the palm of your hand.

4 Carefully press the lower part of each rice ball into the chopped parsley.

5 Spread a little wasabi onto each nigiri rice ball. Place a parsley leaf and then a mussel on top, and press down gently on both.

6 Arrange the mussel nigiri on a bamboo tray, and if you like, serve with soy sauce.

Ingredients

10 large cooked, shelled **mussels**

4 fresh **parsley sprigs**

⅓ cup **sushi rice,** cooked

(see page 9)

1 teaspoon **wasabi paste**

Ingredients

½ ripe **avocado**

1 teaspoon **lemon juice**

2 ounces canned **crabmeat**

1 **carrot**

salt

1 sheet **nori seaweed**

⅓ cup **sushi rice**, cooked
(see page 9)

1 teaspoon **wasabi paste**

2 tablespoons **mayonnaise**

4 tablespoons **sea trout roe**

California Rolls
with Crabmeat

Preparation
MAKES 12 ROLLS

1 Peel and pit the avocado, cut the flesh into thin slices, and sprinkle with lemon juice. Drain the crabmeat and cut it into ¼-inch thick sticks.

2 Rinse and peel the carrot, cut into ¼-inch thick sticks, and blanch in lightly salted boiling water.

3 Cut the sheet of nori in half, cover each piece with half of the rice, and press down firmly. Cover with plastic wrap, and lay a sushi rolling mat on top. Turn over, so that the nori is at the top and the plastic wrap and mat are underneath.

4 Spread some wasabi onto the nori. Lay the avocado slices, carrot sticks, and crayfish or shrimp on top, and add some mayonnaise. Use the plastic wrap and mat to roll up tightly. Cut each roll into 6 pieces of equal size, and garnish the rolls with the fish roe.

Chicken Satay
with Peanut Sauce

Finger food Asian-style: Whether you eat them as an appetizer or an entrée, these spicy satay skewers bring a touch of Thai sophistication to your table

Ingredients

2 skinless, boneless

chicken breast portions

4 **garlic cloves**

2 **lemongrass stalks**

½-inch piece of fresh

ginger root

scant ½ cup **light soy sauce**

grated rind of 1 **lemon**

2 tablespoons **apple juice**

10 **coriander seeds**

1 **star anise** · 1 tablespoon **butter**

10 **black peppercorns**

2 tablespoons **peanut butter**

1 tablespoon **wine vinegar**

pinch of **paprika**

2 tablespoons **heavy cream**

salt · **pepper**

Preparation
SERVES 4

1 Rinse the chicken and pat dry. Trim off any excess fat and cut the flesh into cubes. Place in a nonmetallic dish.

2 Peel and finely chop the garlic and add to the chicken. Rinse and slice the lemongrass. Peel and slice the ginger.

3 Combine the soy sauce, lemon rind, lemongrass, ginger, apple juice, coriander, and star anise, add to the chicken, cover, and marinate for about 4 hours, turning occasionally.

4 Preheat the oven to 175°F. Thread the chicken, lemongrass, and ginger alternately onto wooden skewers. Reserve the marinade. Melt the butter in a skillet, add the peppercorns, and cook the skewered chicken on all sides until tender and golden. Remove from the skillet and keep warm in the oven.

5 Stir the peanut butter into the juices left in the skillet, then stir in scant 1 cup water and the reserved marinade. Stir in the vinegar, paprika, and cream and season with salt and pepper. Sprinkle the sauce with roasted peanuts, if you like, and serve with the skewered chicken.

If you like, you can marinate the skewered chicken overnight. It will keep in the refrigerator in its marinade for a day, by which time it will have fully absorbed all the spicy flavors.

Noodles & Rice

Rice Noodles
with Monkfish and Mushrooms

This will make you long for the sea: When combined with sophisticated monkfish fillet, rice noodles are not out of place even in gourmet circles

Ingredients

2 garlic cloves

1-inch piece of fresh ginger root

1 fresh red chile

2 cups shiitake mushrooms

1 bunch of scallions

9 ounces rice noodles

salt

2 tablespoons sliced almonds

1¼ pounds monkfish fillet

3 tablespoons oil

2 tablespoons sesame oil

2 tablespoons soy sauce

scant 1 cup Chinese rice wine

2 tablespoons fresh

cilantro leaves

Preparation
SERVES 4

1 Peel and finely chop the garlic and ginger. Halve the chile lengthwise, seed, rinse, and cut the flesh into rings. Remove and discard the stems from the shiitake mushrooms, wipe the caps, and slice. Rinse the scallions, then slice diagonally into pieces about ¾ inch long. Cook the rice noodles in lightly salted, boiling water according to the package instructions, until they are tender. Drain, rinse under cold running water, and let drain.

2 Roast the sliced almonds in a dry wok or skillet, stirring frequently, until golden yellow. Remove from the wok or skillet and set aside. Rinse the fish, pat dry, and cut into 8 thick slices. Heat 2 tablespoons of the oil in the preheated wok or skillet, add the monkfish slices, and cook over high heat for about 1 minute on each side. Remove and keep warm.

3 Add the remaining oil to the wok or skillet and heat. Add the garlic, ginger, chile, mushrooms, and scallions, and stir-fry for 2 minutes. Add the noodles, almonds, sesame oil, soy sauce, rice wine, and monkfish. Heat through briefly, then season, and serve immediately, sprinkled with cilantro leaves.

If you can't obtain monkfish, you can use another firm-textured white fish. Make sure that you remove any remaining bones before slicing the fillets. Swordfish or barracuda would be just as sophisticated.

Rice Noodles
with Leeks and Peanuts

In Asia, noodles are said to bring good luck: No wonder there are so
many delicious wok recipes using noodles in Far Eastern cookery

Ingredients

4½ ounces wide **rice noodles**

salt

7 ounces **carrots**

11 ounces **leeks**

1 **garlic clove**

½-inch piece of fresh

ginger root

3 tablespoons **oil**

2 tablespoons roasted

salted peanuts

pepper

Preparation
SERVES 4

1 Cook the rice noodles in lightly salted, boiling water according to
the package instructions, until they are tender. Drain, rinse under
cold running water, and let drain.

2 Peel the carrots and cut into long, thin strips. Wash the leeks
thoroughly and cut into long, thin strips. Peel and finely chop
the garlic and ginger.

3 Heat the oil in a preheated wok or skillet, add the ginger and
garlic, and stir-fry for 5 minutes, until golden. Add the strips of
carrot and leek, and stir-fry for 5 minutes more.

4 Add the noodles and peanuts to the wok or skillet, and stir-fry
for about 2 minutes more, until heated through and thoroughly
combined. Season with salt and pepper and serve immediately.

**"Vegetable noodles" look attractive and
are very easy to make. Simply keep on
peeling the carrots with a vegetable
peeler to make thin ribbons. For leeks,
use a knife to cut them into fine strips.**

Asian Noodles
with Crabmeat

Preparation
SERVES 4

1 Break the noodles into several pieces, and cook in lightly salted, boiling water according to the package instructions, until tender. Drain, rinse under cold running water, and let drain.

2 Rinse the cucumber, halve lengthwise, and scoop out the seeds with a teaspoon. Cut both halves into thin, 3-inch long strips. Wash and slice the star fruit. Halve the chiles lengthwise, seed, rinse, and finely dice the flesh. Break the crabmeat into bitesize pieces.

3 Roast the sesame seeds in a dry wok or skillet, stirring frequently, then remove from the pan. Heat the oil in the wok or skillet, add the chiles and cucumber, and stir-fry for 2 minutes. Add the star fruit and stir-fry for 1–2 minutes more.

4 Add the lime juice, crabmeat, and noodles, stir well, and heat through. Season with salt, sprinkle with the roasted sesame seeds, and serve immediately, garnished with lime wedges if you like.

Ingredients

7 ounces thin **rice noodles**

salt

1 small **cucumber**

2 **star fruit**

2 fresh **red chiles**

11 ounces fresh, frozen and thawed, or canned and drained **crabmeat**

2 tablespoons **sesame seeds**

6 tablespoons **oil**

juice of 2 **limes**

Ingredients

7 ounces **Chinese wheat noodles** · **salt**

1½ cups **shiitake mushrooms**

3 tablespoons **oil** · 4 **scallions**

1 **carrot** · 2 cups **spinach leaves**

2 cups **bean sprouts**

5 ounces **smoked turkey breast**

For the dressing:

1 teaspoon **soy sauce**

2 tablespoons **dry sherry** · **pepper**

1 tablespoon grated fresh **ginger root**

1 tablespoon **walnut oil**

1 tablespoon chopped fresh **cilantro**

2 tablespoons chopped **cashew nuts**

Noodle Salad
with Smoked Turkey

Preparation
SERVES 4

1 Bring the noodles just to a boil in lightly salted water, remove from the heat, and let swell for about 5 minutes. Drain, rinse under cold running water, and let drain.

2 Wipe the mushrooms and cut into fourths. Heat the oil in a wok and stir-fry the mushrooms for 2–3 minutes.

3 Rinse the scallions and thinly slice diagonally. Peel the carrot and cut into thin batons. Wash the spinach leaves

cut into wide strips. Combine the scallions, carrot, spinach, mushrooms, and bean sprouts with the noodles in a bowl. Thinly slice the smoked turkey.

4 Whisk all the dressing ingredients together and pour over the salad. Toss lightly and leave to steep for about 5 minutes. Divide the salad among individual serving plates, place the turkey slices on top, and sprinkle with the cilantro and cashew nuts.

Egg Noodles
with Fish Curry

The perfect match: Chinese egg noodles combine with
tender fish fillets in a fiery yet creamy coconut sauce

Ingredients

5 ounces **Chinese egg noodles**

salt

14 ounces **white fish fillets**

(such as monkfish, halibut, cod)

1¾ cups **shiitake mushrooms**

1 fresh **red chile**

1 tablespoon **oil**

2 tablespoons **curry paste**

1¼ cups **fish stock**

1¾ cups unsweetened

coconut milk

1 teaspoon **cornstarch**

2 tablespoons **Thai fish sauce**

juice of 1 **lemon**

fresh **cilantro leaves**

Preparation
SERVES 4

1 Cook the noodles in lightly salted, boiling water according to the package instructions, until they are tender. Drain, rinse under cold running water, and let drain.

2 Rinse the fish, pat dry, and cut into bitesize pieces. Wipe and slice the mushrooms. Rinse the chile and cut into thin rings.

3 Heat the oil in a preheated wok or pan. Add the mushrooms and stir-fry for 2 minutes. Stir the curry paste into ¼ cup of the fish stock, then add to the mushrooms, together with the remaining fish stock and the coconut milk. Bring to a boil, lower the heat, add the fish, and simmer for 2–3 minutes. Combine the cornstarch with 1 tablespoon water to a smooth paste in a small bowl, add to the curry, and stir in. Season well with salt, Thai fish sauce, and lemon juice. Then add the noodles, and heat through.

4 Spoon the fish curry onto warm plates or into bowls, sprinkle with the chile rings and cilantro leaves, and serve immediately.

Curry paste is available in several varieties. The hottest is red, and its main ingredient is red chiles. There are herbs as well as chiles in the green paste, while the yellow one contains galangal.

Chinese Noodles
with Beef

In China, noodle dishes have probably existed for longer than in Italy:
This particular variation comes with crunchy vegetables and spicy beef

Ingredients

7 ounces Chinese egg noodles

salt

11 ounces round or sirloin steak

1 fresh red chile

3 garlic cloves

3 large bok choy leaves

4 tablespoons oil

1 teaspoon mustard seeds

1¼ cups vegetable stock

3 tablespoons soy sauce

pepper

Preparation
SERVES 4

1 Cook the noodles in lightly salted, boiling water according to the package instructions, until they are tender. Drain, rinse under cold running water, and let drain.

2 Cut the steak into, thin, bitesize pieces. Halve the chile lengthwise, seed, rinse, and finely dice. Peel and slice the garlic. Rinse the bok choy leaves. Cut out the white stalks, cut them into pieces about ¾ inch wide. Shred the green parts.

3 Heat the oil in a preheated wok or skillet. Add the mustard seeds, garlic, and chile, and stir-fry for 1 minute. Add the white pieces of bok choy and the meat, lower the heat, and stir-fry briefly, but do not let brown. Add the vegetable stock and soy sauce, cover, and cook for 3 minutes over low heat, then add the green bok choy strips. Re-cover and simmer for 7 minutes more. Season with salt and pepper, add the noodles, and heat through. Serve hot.

Instead of bok choy, try different vegetables, such as broccoli, bell peppers, or Savoy cabbage. Lightly roasted cashew nuts or peanuts will give this noodle dish some extra punch.

Vegetable Kabobs
with Glass Noodles

Preparation

MAKES 16 KABOBS

1 Rinse the vegetables, wipe the mushrooms, and drain the bean curd. Cut the vegetables and the bean curd into large chunks. Thread alternately onto wooden skewers.

2 Spread out the seasoned flour on a plate and turn the skewers in it. Shake off any excess flour.

3 Combine the cornstarch, baking powder, and tandoori paste and stir in 5 tablespoons water. In another bowl beat the egg whites to soft peaks and fold in.

4 Heat the oil in a wok or a deep-fryer to 350°F. Coat the kabobs in the egg white batter, and deep-fry, one at a time, for about 3 minutes. Break the glass noodles into smaller pieces and deep-fry for 1–2 minutes.

5 For the dipping sauce, halve the chile lengthwise, seed, rinse, and slice. Rinse the scallion and cut into rings. Combine with the rice vinegar. Arrange the vegetable kabobs on a bed of deep-fried glass noodles, and serve with the dipping sauce.

Ingredients

2 bunches of **scallions**

1 **red**, 1 **yellow**, and 1 **green bell pepper**

1 **eggplant** · 1 small **Chinese cabbage**

1½ cups **mushrooms**

3½ ounces firm **bean curd**

¾ cup seasoned **all-purpose flour**

⅓ cup **cornstarch** · 1 teaspoon **baking powder**

½ teaspoon **tandoori paste** · 2 **egg whites**

4 cups **oil**, for deep-frying

9 ounces **glass noodles**

For the dipping sauce:

1 fresh **chile** · ½ **scallion**

¼ cup **rice vinegar**

Ingredients

7 ounces skinless, boneless

chicken breast portion

2 **eggs** · 1 cup cooked peeled **shrimp**

2 ounces **leaf spinach**, thawed if frozen

½ cup cooked **short grain rice**

1 tablespoon unsweetened **coconut milk**

grated rind of ½ **lemon**

½ fresh **chile** (finely chopped)

salt · **pepper**

3 ounces **rice noodles**

all-purpose flour, for dusting

4 cups **oil**, for deep-frying

Chicken Balls
Coated in Rice Noodles

Preparation
SERVES 4

1 Coarsely chop the chicken, then process in a food processor until very finely ground. Scrape into a bowl, and add 1 egg. Coarsely chop the shrimp and spinach and stir into the chicken mixture with the rice. Add the coconut milk, lemon rind, and chile, and season to taste with salt and pepper.

2 Lightly beat the second egg in a shallow dish. Cut up the rice noodles and set aside in another shallow dish.

3 With damp hands, form the chicken mixture into walnut-size balls, then coat first in the flour, then in the beaten egg, and finally in the rice noodles. Press the outer coating on firmly.

4 Heat the oil in a wok or deep-fryer to 350°F, then drop in the chicken balls, one at a time, and deep-fry for 3–4 minutes, until golden brown and crisp. A spicy pineapple chutney would go well with this dish.

Basmati Rice
with Spices

An exclusive dish in record time: Fragrant basmati rice
together with aromatic spices and sweet raisins make for a dream team

Ingredients

3 tablespoons **raisins**

⅔ cup **basmati rice**

salt · pepper

1 **cardamom pod** · 1 **clove**

pinch of **saffron powder**

pinch of **ground cinnamon**

1 **lime**

scant ¼ cup sliced **almonds**

Preparation
SERVES 2

1 Place the raisins in a small bowl, cover with lukewarm water, and set aside to soak. Place the rice in a strainer and rinse under cold running water until the water runs clear.

2 Pour 1¼ cups water into a pan, add salt, pepper, the cardamom pod, clove, saffron, and cinnamon, and bring to a boil. Add the rice, cover, and simmer gently for about 10 minutes. Turn off the heat and leave the rice, still covered, for 10 minutes to swell.

3 Wash and dry the lime, then cut it in half crosswise. Squeeze the juice from one half, and thinly slice the other. Roast the almonds in a dry skillet, stirring frequently, until golden. Drain the raisins. Stir the almonds, raisins and lime juice into the rice. Serve garnished with lime slices.

True rice fans will eat this spicy rice on its own, but it is also a delicious accompaniment to chicken curry with coconut milk, as well as sweet and sour lamb, and vegetable dishes.

Saffron Rice
with Vegetables

A culinary performance with three leading roles: Exotic spices,
vegetables, and basmati rice combine to create an irresistible dish

Ingredients

2 tablespoons **cashew nuts**

1 **cinnamon stick**

6 green **cardamom pods**

4 **cloves** · 2 **bay leaves**

11 ounces **carrots**

9 ounces **Savoy cabbage**

(or leeks)

1 teaspoon **saffron powder**

2 tablespoons **oil**

1¼ cups **basmati rice**

1¼ cups **peas** (frozen)

2½ cups **vegetable stock** · salt

11 ounces fresh **leaf spinach**

pepper

Preparation
SERVES 4

1 Coarsely chop the cashew nuts. Roast the nuts in a dry skillet until golden. Remove from the skillet and set aside. In turn, dry-fry the spices until they give off a fragrance. Let cool.

2 Peel and finely dice the carrots. Rinse the cabbage or leeks, then cut into strips or rings. Combine the saffron with 2 tablespoons hot water in a small bowl.

3 Heat the oil in a preheated wok or a deep skillet. Briefly stir-fry the rice, carrots, and cabbage or leeks. Add the nuts, spices, peas, and saffron liquid. Pour in the stock and season with salt. Bring to a boil, cover, and cook for 15 minutes over low heat.

4 Meanwhile rinse the spinach and drain thoroughly. Add the spinach to the rice and cook for about 5 minutes more, until the rice is soft. Season with salt and pepper and serve.

You can vary the vegetables according to what is available—broccoli, bok choy, and bell peppers would also go well with saffron rice. Unsalted peanuts can be used instead of cashews.

Exotic Fried Rice
with Shrimp

Preparation
SERVES 4

1 Rinse the scallions, and cut into thick slices on the diagonal. Peel and pit the mango, then cut the flesh into small cubes.

2 Rinse and finely chop the lemongrass. Peel and finely chop the garlic. Heat the oil in a preheated wok or a deep, heavy skillet. Add the lemongrass and garlic and stir-fry over medium heat for about 1 minute.

3 Add the scallions and mango, season with cumin, cinnamon, cayenne pepper, and curry powder, and stir-fry for a few minutes. Pour in the sherry, bring to a boil, and boil vigorously for 1–2 minutes.

4 Mix in the rice, bean sprouts, and shrimp, heat through, stirring occasionally, for a few minutes, then serve sprinkled with cilantro leaves.

52

Ingredients

1 bunch of **scallions**

½ ripe **mango**

2 **lemongrass stalks**

1 **garlic clove** · 2 tablespoons **oil**

1 pinch each of **ground cumin, ground cinnamon,** and **cayenne pepper**

1 teaspoon **curry powder**

3 tablespoons **dry sherry**

2⅓ cups cooked **basmati rice**

1 cup **bean sprouts**

1¾ cups cooked, peeled **shrimp**

2 tablespoons **cilantro leaves**

Ingredients

2 **duck breast fillets** (7 ounces each)

salt · **pepper**

2 tablespoons **oil**

1 **leek** · 2 **carrots**

½ **pineapple**

1 fresh **red chile**

1 tablespoon grated fresh **ginger root**

2⅓ cups cooked **long grain rice**

2 tablespoons **soy sauce**

1 tablespoon **dry sherry**

5 tablespoons **chicken stock**

Asian Fried Rice
with Duck Breast

Preparation
SERVES 4

1 Preheat the oven to 350°F. Rinse the duck and pat dry, then season with salt and pepper. Heat the oil in a skillet, add the duck, skin side down, and cook over high heat for 3–4 minutes, until browned. Turn and cook for 4–5 minutes more. Place in an ovenproof dish, skin side up, and roast for about 10 minutes, until tender.

2 Rinse the leek and slice into thin rings. Peel the carrots and slice into thin strips. Peel, core, and dice the pineapple. Halve the chile lengthwise, seed, rinse, and cut the flesh into strips.

3 Cook the leek, carrots, and pineapple in the fat remaining in the skillet, stirring occasionally until softened. Add the chile, ginger, and rice and stir well to mix. Season with soy sauce, sherry, and stock. Cut the pink duck breast meat into thin slices and mix in with the rice. Heat through gently, then serve.

Nasi Goreng
with Fried Eggs

A **classic** of Asian cookery: Cooking Indonesian fried rice will give free rein to your imagination—anything goes as long as it tastes **good**

Ingredients

1½ cups **long grain rice** · **salt**

1 bunch of **scallions**

12 ounces **pork tenderloin**

4 **shallots**

2 **garlic cloves**

6 tablespoons **oil** · 4 **eggs**

pepper

2 tablespoons **kecap benteng**

1 teaspoon **sambal oelek**

pinch of **ground galangal**

Preparation
SERVES 4

1   Rinse the rice under cold running water, drain, and place in a pan with 2¼ cups water and 1 teaspoon salt. Bring to a boil, lower the heat, cover, and simmer for about 20 minutes. Fluff up the rice with a fork and let stand, uncovered, to cool.

2   Rinse the scallions. Cut the white parts lengthwise into fourths, then slice diagonally into pieces about 1½ inches long. Thinly slice the pork tenderloin, then cut into strips. Peel and thinly slice the shallots. Peel and finely chop the garlic.

3   Heat 3 tablespoons of the oil in a preheated wok until very hot. Separate half the shallot slices into rings and cook in the hot oil, turning frequently, until golden brown and crisp. Remove with a slotted spoon and drain on paper towels. Add 2 tablespoons of the remaining oil to the wok and stir-fry the strips of meat for about 5 minutes, until crisp.

4   Add the remaining shallots, the garlic, and scallions and stir-fry for 2–3 minutes. Finally, add the rice and cook over high heat, stirring constantly, for 3–5 minutes, until golden. Meanwhile, heat the remaining oil in a skillet and fry the eggs, seasoning each egg white with a little salt and pepper.

5   Quickly mix the fried rice with the kecap benteng, sambal oelek, and galangal, season with salt and pepper, and arrange on plates. Place a fried egg on top of each portion of nasi goreng and sprinkle with the crisp-fried shallots before serving.

Fish & Meat

Seafood Curry
with Shrimp and Mango

Elegant seafood in a fruity combination: Two very different taste sensations
make this curry an extravagant feast for the taste buds

Ingredients

1¼ pounds frozen **seafood**

(such as shrimp, mussels, squid)

2 **mangoes**

3 tablespoons **grated coconut**

3 tablespoons unsweetened

coconut milk

2 pinches **chili powder**

2 tablespoons **curry powder**

1 large **carrot** · 2 **onions**

3 **garlic cloves** · 2 **celery stalks**

2 tablespoons **oil**

juice of ½ **lemon**

5 tablespoons **sesame oil**

salt · pepper

Preparation
SERVES 4

1 Thaw the seafood, then rinse under cold running water, and pat
dry with paper towels.

2 Peel the mangoes and cut the flesh away from the pit in slices
about ¼ inch thick. Place half the flesh in a blender with the
grated coconut, coconut milk, chili powder, curry powder, and
3 tablespoons water and process until smooth.

3 Peel and finely dice the carrot, onions, and garlic. Rinse and
finely dice the celery stalks. Reserve some of the green celery
leaves for the garnish.

4 Heat the oil in a preheated wok or skillet, add the diced
vegetables, and stir-fry until softened. Add the seafood and stir-
fry briefly. Stir in the mango mixture and simmer over low heat
for about 8 minutes. If the sauce seems too thick, add a little
extra coconut milk or water.

5 Season the curry with the lemon juice, sesame oil, salt, and
pepper, and serve garnished with the remaining mango slices
and the reserved celery leaves.

**Instead of using a mixture of seafood
for this curry, you can make it with
jumbo shrimp alone. As well as the
frozen shrimp, you can buy them either
cooked (pink) or raw (gray or blue).**

Garlic Shrimp
with Pineapple

For special occasions: Crisp, deep-fried shrimp are arranged
decoratively with an aromatic sauce in hollowed-out pineapple

Ingredients

1 egg white

4 teaspoons cornstarch

1 teaspoon grated fresh

ginger root

1 teaspoon soy sauce

1 teaspoon curry powder

4–5 garlic cloves · salt

1¼ pounds cooked peeled shrimp

2 small pineapples

3 tablespoons white

wine vinegar

1½ teaspoons sugar

2 tablespoons kecap manis

cayenne pepper

5 tablespoons vegetable stock

3½ cups oil, for deep frying

1 tablespoon chopped

fresh cilantro

Preparation
SERVES 4

1   Beat the egg white in a large dish until foamy. Gradually stir in
    half the cornstarch, then the ginger, soy sauce, and curry powder.
    Peel and coarsely chop the garlic, then stir into the mixture.
    Season with salt. Add the shrimp, cover with plastic wrap, and
    marinate for 30 minutes.

2   Halve the pineapples lengthwise and hollow out the flesh, leaving
    thick shells. Dice the flesh on a plate to catch the juice, then
    drain it into a bowl.

3   Measure 5 tablespoons of the pineapple juice into a pan with the
    vinegar, sugar, kecap manis, cayenne pepper, vegetable stock, and
    remaining cornstarch, stir until smooth, and bring to a boil.

4   Heat the oil to 300°F in a large pan or deep-fryer. Drop in the
    shrimp and deep-fry for 1–2 minutes. Remove with a slotted
    spoon and drain on paper towels.

5   Heat 2 tablespoons of the deep-frying oil in a wok or skillet.
    Briefly stir-fry the shrimp, then stir in the pineapple pieces and
    the sauce. Pile the shrimp into the hollowed-out pineapple shells,
    and sprinkle with the cilantro before serving.

**If you need to prepare this quickly, you
can use 7 ounces canned pineapple
instead of fresh, reserving the can juice
for making the sauce. In that case, serve
the garlic shrimp in small bowls.**

Squid
with Sugar-snap Peas

For those who love the delights of the sea: Tender squid cooked
in a wok with crunchy sugar-snap peas, garlic, and spices

Ingredients

14 ounces prepared **squid**

salt · 2⅔ cups **sugar-snap peas**

14 ounces **green bell peppers**

2 tablespoons **sesame oil**

3 chopped **garlic cloves**

2 teaspoons grated fresh

ginger root

4 tablespoons **light soy sauce**

6 tablespoons **oyster sauce**

4 tablespoons **Chinese rice wine**

½ cup **chicken stock**

1½ tablespoons **cornstarch**

Preparation
SERVES 4

1 Rinse the squid under cold running water, pat dry, and cut
lengthwise into thin strips. Blanch briefly in lightly salted,
boiling water and drain well.

2 Rinse the sugar-snap peas. Halve the bell peppers lengthwise,
seed, rinse, and cut the flesh into narrow strips.

3 Heat the oil in a preheated wok or a large skillet. Add the garlic
and ginger and stir-fry for 1 minute. Add the sugar-snap peas and
strips of green bell pepper and stir-fry for 1–2 minutes more.

4 Pour in the soy sauce, oyster sauce, rice wine, and stock and cook
gently for 1 minute. Mix the cornstarch with 3 tablespoons cold
water to a smooth paste, stir into the wok, and bring to a boil.

5 Add the squid, mix well, bring back to a boil, and season. Serve
immediately. Basmati rice would go well with this dish.

**If you want to add more color, it's very
simple—use red or yellow bell peppers
instead of green. If sugar-snap peas
aren't available, you can blanch green
beans or broccoli flowerets.**

Squid
on a Bed of Vegetables

Preparation
SERVES 2

1 Rinse the squid and pat dry. Cut the body sacs open, score diamond shapes into the flesh, and cut into pieces.

2 Rinse the sugar-snap peas. Halve the bell peppers lengthwise, seed, rinse, and cut the flesh into strips. Rinse the cucumber, halve it lengthwise, scoop out the seeds, and cut the flesh into thin strips. Peel and finely chop the garlic. Halve the chiles lengthwise, seed, rinse, and chop finely. Wash the basil, shake dry, and pull off the leaves. Blanch the bean sprouts for about 2 minutes.

3 Heat 2 tablespoons oil in a preheated wok or skillet. Stir-fry the squid for 1 minute. Add the chiles and garlic and stir-fry for 5 minutes. Stir in the lime juice and soy sauce. Remove the mixture from the pan and keep warm.

4 Heat the remaining oil and stir-fry the sugar-snap peas and bell pepper for 1–2 minutes. Add the strips of cucumber and the bean sprouts and stir-fry for 1–2 minutes more. Return the squid mixture to the pan to heat through and stir in the basil leaves before serving.

Ingredients

1¼ pounds prepared **squid**

1¾ cups **sugar-snap peas**

1 **yellow** and 1 **red bell pepper**

7 ounces **cucumber**

3 **garlic cloves**

2 fresh **red chiles**

1 bunch of **Thai basil**

1¾ cups **bean sprouts**

5 tablespoons **peanut oil**

3 tablespoons **lime juice**

4 tablespoons **light soy sauce**

Ingredients

24 large **spinach leaves**

salt

9 ounces very fresh **tuna fillet**

1 teaspoon **wasabi paste**

For the tempura batter:

scant ½ cup **cornstarch**

1 teaspoon **baking powder**

2 **egg whites**

4 cups **oil**, for deep-frying

Tuna
Coated in Spinach and Tempura

Preparation
SERVES 4

1 Briefly blanch the spinach leaves, one at a time, in lightly salted, boiling water. Remove with a slotted spoon, spread out on a board, and cut out the stalks. Cut the fish into four equal pieces and spread with wasabi.

2 For each serving, arrange six spinach leaves on top of one another so that they overlap, then place one piece of tuna on each stack of leaves. Fold the leaves in at the ends and roll up with the filling.

3 For the tempura batter, combine the cornstarch and baking powder in a bowl and stir in about 5 tablespoons cold water. Beat the egg whites in another bowl until soft peaks form, then fold into the mixture. Heat the oil in a wok or deep-fryer to 350°F. One at a time, dip the filled spinach rolls in the batter to coat, then fry in the hot oil for about 3 minutes, until they are golden brown. Drain well, cut through the rolls diagonally, and if you like, serve with caviar and grated radish.

Chicken Laksa
with vegetables

Wonderfully aromatic: Instead of fish, this typically Malayan stew
is full of tender chicken in a creamy sauce

Ingredients

1 garlic clove · 1 small onion

¼ bunch of fresh cilantro

2 fresh green chiles

1 teaspoon peanut oil

½ teaspoon shrimp paste

2 skinless, boneless

chicken breast portions

2 ounces thin rice noodles

1 tablespoon sesame oil

1 tablespoon soy sauce

1 tablespoon coconut cream

4 tablespoons unsweetened

coconut milk

1¾ cups chicken stock

2 limes · 1 cup bean sprouts

1 handful Chinese

flowering cabbage

½ red bell pepper (cut in strips)

2 scallions

Preparation
SERVES 2

1 Peel and coarsely chop the garlic and onion. Rinse the cilantro, shake dry, reserve a few leaves for the garnish, and coarsely chop the remainder. Halve the chiles lengthwise, seed, and rinse. Place all of these in a blender, add the peanut oil and shrimp paste, and process to a fine paste. Scrape into a bowl.

2 Rinse the chicken and pat dry. Coat the chicken with half the spice paste. Place on a plate, cover with plastic wrap, and marinate in the refrigerator for 3–4 hours.

3 Cut the rice noodles into shorter lengths with scissors, place in a bowl, pour in hot water to cover, and leave to swell.

4 Heat the sesame oil in a skillet. Add the chicken and brown on both sides. Add the remaining spice paste, the soy sauce, coconut cream, coconut milk, and stock. Squeeze the juice and grate the rind of one lime and add to the skillet. Cook gently for about 8–10 minutes. Drain the noodles and add to the skillet with the bean sprouts, and Chinese flowering cabbage leaves. Cook for about 1 minute more.

5 Rinse the scallions and cut into strips. Rinse, dry and slice the second lime. Divide the noodles among two bowls and pour over some of the sauce and vegetables. Arrange the chicken on top with the remaining vegetables and serve garnished with strips of red bell pepper, scallions, lime slices, and the reserved cilantro.

Fragrant Chicken

Sweet and Sour

Chicken can be so seductive—in this typically Asian recipe
it is fried with fragrant pineapple and spicy-hot ginger

Ingredients

1-inch piece of fresh **ginger root**

2 **garlic cloves**

6 tablespoons **light soy sauce**

4 tablespoons **rice vinegar**

1 teaspoon **Chinese**

five-spice powder

1¼ pounds skinless, boneless

chicken breast portions

1 bunch of **scallions**

4 **carrots** · ¼ **pineapple**

2 tablespoons **oil**

1¾ cups **chicken stock**

3 tablespoons **tomato paste**

2 teaspoons **cornstarch** · **salt**

pepper · **sugar**

Preparation

SERVES 4

1 Peel and finely dice the ginger and garlic. Combine the ginger and garlic with the soy sauce, rice vinegar, and five-spice powder in a shallow dish. Rinse the chicken, pat dry, and cut into bitesize pieces. Add to the dish, turning to coat, cover with plastic wrap, and marinate for 30 minutes.

2 Rinse the scallions and slice diagonally into thin rings. Peel the carrots and cut into thin sticks. Peel and core the pineapple and dice the flesh.

3 Heat the oil in a preheated wok or skillet. Drain the chicken, reserving the marinade, add to the wok or skillet, and stir-fry over medium heat for 5 minutes, until browned on all sides. Add the scallions and carrot sticks and stir-fry for 2–3 minutes more.

4 Whisk the reserved marinade with the stock, tomato paste, and cornstarch, add to the wok or skillet, and bring to a boil. Stir in the pineapple pieces, season to taste with salt, pepper, and sugar, and cook gently for a few minutes, until heated through. Serve immediately. Basmati rice would go well with this dish.

This dish is not just for guests: Instead of chicken, use skinless aromatic duck breast fillet. Cut the duck into narrow strips and cook over high heat for just a short time, so that the meat is still pink inside.

Chicken Curry
Indian Style

Preparation
SERVES 4

1 Rinse the chicken, pat dry, and cut into thin strips. Combine the lemon rind and juice, sambal oelek, sugar, salt, pepper, and coriander in a shallow dish. Add the chicken, turn to coat, then marinate for 20 minutes.

2 Rinse the scallions and separate the white and green parts. Cut the white parts lengthwise into fourths, and cut both green and white parts into 1-inch long pieces. Rinse and halve the beans and cook in lightly salted, boiling water for 10 minutes. Drain, rinse, and drain again.

3 Drain the chicken, reserving the marinade. Heat the oil in a preheated wok or skillet and stir-fry the chicken for 5 minutes, until browned all over. Add the scallions and garlic and stir-fry for 2 minutes. Add the ginger, garam masala, curry powder, the reserved marinade, and the coconut milk and cook gently for about 5 minutes.

4 Add the beans and adjust the seasoning if necessary. Serve garnished with cilantro leaves. Indian poppadums would go well with this dish.

Ingredients

4 small skinless, boneless

chicken breast portions

grated rind and juice of ½ **lemon**

1 teaspoon **sambal oelek**

1 teaspoon **sugar · salt · pepper**

½ teaspoon **ground coriander**

3 **scallions · 11 ounces green beans**

4 tablespoons **sesame oil · 2 garlic cloves**

1 teaspoon grated fresh **ginger root**

1 teaspoon **garam masala**

1 tablespoon **curry powder**

1⅔ cups unsweetened **coconut milk**

fresh **cilantro leaves**, to garnish

Ingredients

9 ounces **green Japanese noodles**

1 tablespoon **honey**

4 tablespoons **soy sauce**

½ teaspoon **sambal oelek**

2 **duck breast fillets**

(about 1 pound 5 ounces)

3 tablespoons **oil** · **salt**

2 tablespoons **lemon juice**

¼ cup **chicken stock**

1 **scallion**

Duck Breast Strips
on Green Noodles

Preparation
SERVES 4

1 Cook the noodles in lightly salted, boiling water according to the package instructions, until tender. Drain, rinse under cold running water, and let drain.

2 Combine the honey, soy sauce, and sambal oelek in a large shallow dish. Slice the duck breasts and add to the dish, turning to coat. Cover with plastic wrap and marinate for 30 minutes. Drain the duck thoroughly and reserve the marinade.

3 Heat the oil in a preheated wok or skillet. Add the duck and cook until browned all over. Season with salt and lemon juice. Remove from the pan and keep warm. Pour in the stock and the reserved marinade, add the noodles, and cook until tender.

4 Rinse the scallion and slice thinly. Shape the noodles into nests on serving plates and top with the duck. Garnish with the scallion and, if you like, shiso leaves.

Lamb Curry
with Spinach

A classic Indian combination: Tender lamb braised
with spices and spinach and topped with fresh yogurt

Ingredients

1 pound 5 ounces **leaf spinach**

14 ounces **lamb** (loin or leg)

4 **onions** · 2 **garlic cloves**

1-inch piece of fresh **ginger root**

2 tablespoons **oil**

½ teaspoon **chili powder**

1 teaspoon each **ground cumin**,

cardamom, and **coriander**

1 teaspoon **garam masala**

½ teaspoon **fenugreek seeds**

¼ teaspoon **cayenne pepper**

scant 1 cup **plain yogurt** · **salt**

Preparation
SERVES 4

1 Rinse the spinach and remove any tough stalks. Place the leaves in a bowl, pour in boiling water to cover, and let stand for 1 minute. Drain, rinse with cold water, and let drain.

2 Cut the lamb into bitesize cubes. Peel the onions and garlic and cut into strips. Peel and finely chop the ginger.

3 Heat the oil in a preheated wok or a wide skillet. Add the onion and stir-fry for 2–3 minutes. Add the lamb, ginger, and garlic and stir-fry until the meat is browned all over.

4 Stir in the spices and stir-fry for 1 minute. Pour in 1¼ cups water, cover, and cook over low heat, stirring occasionally, for 20 minutes. Add the spinach, re-cover, and cook for 10 minutes more. Finally, remove the lid and cook over high heat for 5 minutes, until the sauce thickens.

5 Stir the yogurt until creamy, then stir most of it into the curry. Season with salt and heat gently, but do not let the mixture boil. Transfer the curry to a serving dish, spoon the remaining yogurt on top, and serve. Basmati rice would go well with this dish.

Stir-fry
with Pork Tenderloin

Very little effort for a big effect: This stir-fry takes no time to make, and tastes so incredibly good that you can't get enough of it

Ingredients

14 ounces **pork tenderloin**

3 tablespoons **oyster sauce**

½ teaspoon **pepper**

2¼ cups drained canned

bamboo shoots

3½ ounces fresh **leaf spinach**

5 tablespoons **sesame oil**

1 tablespoon **yellow curry paste**

2 teaspoons **sugar**

2 tablespoons **lime juice**

1 **lime**

Preparation
SERVES 4

1 Cut the pork into bitesize pieces and place in a shallow dish. Add the oyster sauce and pepper, stir well to coat, and marinate for about 15 minutes.

2 Cut the bamboo shoots into thin strips. Rinse the spinach, drain thoroughly, then remove any tough stalks.

3 Heat the oil in a preheated wok or skillet. Drain the pork, then stir-fry over high heat for about 2 minutes, until browned all over. Stir in the curry paste, then add bamboo shoots and spinach. Season with sugar and lime juice and cook, stirring constantly, for 2 minutes more.

4 Rinse and dry the lime, then cut into wedges. Divide the pork mixture among four small bowls and serve garnished with the lime segments. Basmati rice would go well with this dish.

You can, of course, make this stir-fry with other sorts of meat, such as steak. If you do, you should add a hotter note to the flavoring—season, for example, with 1 tablespoon red curry paste.

Beef
with Orange

Preparation
SERVES 2

1 Wash the rice thoroughly, place in a pan, and add 1 cup water and a pinch of salt. Bring to a boil, cover, lower the heat, and simmer for 20 minutes.

2 Rinse and dry the orange, then shave off thin pieces of rind for the garnish. Remove the remaining skin and pith, then cut the orange into segments over a bowl to catch the juice. Rinse and slice the scallions. Cut the steak against the grain into bitesize strips and season with salt and pepper. Heat the oil in a preheated wok or skillet

and stir-fry over high heat for about 3 minutes, until browned. Remove from the pan and keep warm.

3 Add the white parts of the scallions to the wok or skillet and stir-fry for 3–4 minutes. Add all of the orange juice, the soy sauce, and honey and cook until reduced to a syrupy consistency. Season with salt and pepper. Add the orange segments and the steak and heat through. Stir in the green parts of the scallions. Arrange the steak on the rice and sprinkle with the pieces of orange rind.

Ingredients

½ cup **basmati rice**

salt

1 **orange**

2 **scallions**

11 ounces **round** or **sirloin steak**

pepper · 2 tablespoons **sesame oil**

⅔ cup **orange juice**

1 tablespoon **light soy sauce**

1 tablespoon **honey**

Ingredients

1 red bell pepper

4 garlic cloves

6 tablespoons **soy sauce**

4 teaspoons **lime juice**

½ cup **Thai fish sauce**

1 teaspoon **white pepper**

⅔ cup **meat stock**

1 teaspoon **cornstarch**

1¼ pounds **pork tenderloin**

2 tablespoons **oil**

7 ounces **udon noodles** · salt

½ bunch of **scallions**

Pork
in Sweet and Sour Sauce

Preparation
SERVES 4

1 Halve the bell pepper lengthwise, seed, rinse, and finely dice. Peel and finely chop the garlic. Combine the bell pepper, garlic, soy sauce, lime juice, fish sauce, pepper, stock, and cornstarch in a shallow dish. Add the meat, turn to coat, and marinate for 30 minutes.

2 Preheat the oven to 350°F. Drain the pork, reserving the marinade. Heat the oil in a skillet, add the pork, and brown on all sides over medium heat. Transfer the pork to an ovenproof dish and roast for about 15 minutes, until cooked through. Add the reserved marinade to the meat for the last 5 minutes.

3 Cook the noodles in lightly salted, boiling water according to the package instructions. Rinse the scallions and slice the green parts diagonally. Mix the noodles with the sauce, and slice the pork. Arrange the noodles and meat in small bowls, and garnish with the scallions.

Beef
with Scallions

It doesn't always have to be rice: Marinated slices of beef are
served here with ginger-spiced scallions on fine noodles

Ingredients

1¼ pounds **beef tenderloin**

4 tablespoons **oil**

2 tablespoons **soy sauce**

½ teaspoon **pepper**

½ bunch of **scallions**

1 **garlic clove**

7 ounces thin **rice noodles** · salt

1 teaspoon grated fresh

ginger root

4 tablespoons **oyster sauce**

4 tablespoons **Chinese rice wine**

2 tablespoons chopped,

unsalted peanuts

Preparation
SERVES 4

1 Cut the beef against the grain into bitesize slices. Combine
2 tablespoons of the oil, the soy sauce, and pepper in a shallow
dish. Add the beef, turn to coat, cover with plastic wrap, and
marinate for about 30 minutes.

2 Rinse the scallions and separate the green and white parts. Cut the
white parts lengthwise into fourths and slice both the white and
green parts into 1½-inch long pieces. Peel and finely chop the
garlic. Preheat the broiler and oil the broiler pan.

3 Drain the beef and cook under the hot broiler on both sides
until tender.

4 Cook the rice noodles in lightly salted, boiling water according to
the package instructions, until tender. Drain well.

5 Heat the remaining oil in a preheated wok or skillet and stir-fry
the scallions, ginger, and garlic for 2–3 minutes. Add the oyster
sauce and rice wine and cook for about 2 minutes more.

6 Spoon the noodles into small bowls, place the beef and scallions
on top, and sprinkle with the peanuts. If you like, garnish with
cilantro leaves and garlic chives.

**If you're not in a hurry, let the strips of
beef marinate for a little longer—up to
2 hours. They will not only absorb more
flavor, but, at the same time, they will
also become even more tender.**

Asian Fondue
with Meat and Dips

Fondue is a tradition in the Far East: Friends get together to
cook the pieces of meat in stock and dip them in spicy sauces

Ingredients

1 carrot

2-inch piece of fresh ginger root

¾ cup sesame oil · 4 fresh chiles

7 garlic cloves

7 tablespoons soy sauce

6¼ cups chicken or meat stock

¼ teaspoon sesame seeds

1 tablespoon honey

3 tablespoons apple vinegar

1 shallot · juice of 2 limes

4 tablespoons tomato ketchup

salt · ⅓ cup plain yogurt

1 tablespoon mango chutney

1 teaspoon curry powder

1 tablespoon grated coconut

1 tablespoon chopped

fresh cilantro

800 g turkey breast, beef

tenderloin, or loin of veal

Preparation
SERVES 4

1 Peel the carrot and cut into thin strips. Peel the ginger and cut
half of it into thin strips. Place the carrot and ginger strips in a
large pan and add the stock, 5 tablespoons of the sesame oil,
2 chiles, 4 unpeeled garlic cloves, and 4 tablespoons soy sauce.
Cook over low heat for 15 minutes.

2 Meanwhile, put the sesame seeds in a blender with 5 tablespoons
of the remaining sesame oil, the honey, vinegar, and the remaining
soy sauce, and process until smooth to form a sauce.

3 Peel and finely chop the shallot and the remaining garlic. Finely
grate the remaining ginger. Halve the remaining chiles lengthwise,
seed, rinse, and cut into fine strips. Combine the shallot, garlic,
ginger, and chiles with the lime juice and ketchup to form a
sauce. Season with salt.

4 Combine the yogurt with the remaining sesame oil, the mango
chutney, curry powder, grated coconut, and cilantro, to form a
sauce. Season with salt.

5 Cut the meat into ½-inch cubes and place in four individual
dishes. Pour the stock into a fondue pot, bring to the table, and
keep hot. Spoon the sauces into small serving bowls.

6 The diners spear the pieces of meat, one at a time, with fondue
forks and cook for a few minutes in the hot stock. They can then
dip the meat into the sauces.

Desserts

Mango Lassi
with Papaya

Wonderfully refreshing: This delicious drink can be an aperitif, or a dessert after a hot, spicy meal—either way it's a great way for gourmets to get vitamins

Ingredients

1 ripe **papaya**

1 ripe **mango**

2 tablespoons **lime juice**

seeds from ½ **vanilla bean**

2 teaspoons **honey**

1⅔ cup **buttermilk**

4 tablespoons **whole milk yogurt**

Preparation
SERVES 4

1 Halve the papaya and remove and reserve the seeds. Peel the papaya, cut off four slices, and reserve for decoration. Cut the remaining flesh into cubes. Peel the mango, cut the flesh away from the flat, central pit, and dice.

2 Place the mango and papaya flesh in a blender with the lime juice, vanilla seeds, honey, and buttermilk and process to a smooth, foaming purée.

3 Pour the mixture into glasses, then spoon 1 tablespoon yogurt on top of each glass, and sprinkle with a few papaya seeds. Serve garnished with the reserved papaya slices.

You can also make lassi with yogurt. To keep the mixture liquid, just add a little water. A delicious variation is mint lassi: Mix plain yogurt, water, fresh mint leaves, and sugar.

Coconut Rice
with Mango Slices

A tropical finale: The creamy rice has a delicate fragrance of coconut, and the whole dish is rounded off by the fruity flavor of fresh mango

Ingredients

1¼ cups **sticky rice · salt**

pinch of **saffron powder**

2 teaspoons **powdered mango**

½ cup **sugar**

4 cups **coconut cream**

1 ripe **mango**

Preparation
SERVES 4

1 Wash the rice in a strainer under cold running water. Place in a pan with 2½ cups lightly salted water and stir in the saffron powder and powdered mango. Bring to a boil, cover, and simmer over low heat, stirring occasionally, for about 20 minutes. Remove from the heat and stir in the sugar.

2 Add a pinch of salt to the coconut cream, then bring to a boil in another pan over low heat, stirring constantly. Remove from the heat and set aside. Wash and, if you like, peel the mango. Cut the flesh away from the pit into slices.

3 Before serving, arrange the rice decoratively on plates with the coconut cream and mango slices.

Powdered mango gives a rich, fruity aroma not only to desserts, but also to curries. The naturally occurring enzymes in powdered mango also make meat and fish wonderfully tender.

Pear in Plum Wine
with Orange Jelly

Preparation
SERVES 2

1 Soak the gelatin in a small bowl of cold water. Heat the orange juice with the mango syrup in a small pan. Squeeze out the gelatin, add to the pan, and dissolve. Line a small dessert mold with plastic wrap, pour in the mixture, and chill in the refrigerator for 1 hour, until set.

2 Heat the plum wine in a pan. Peel, halve, and core the pear, leaving the stalk intact. Cut into thin slices, leaving them attached at the stalk end. Carefully place the pear halves in the wine and add sufficient hot water to cover them completely. Cook over medium heat until they are tender, but not disintegrating.

3 Turn out and dice the orange jelly. If you like, cut part of the jelly into decorative shapes.

4 Arrange the pear halves on serving plates in a fan shape and garnish with the jelly.

Ingredients

3 **white gelatin leaves**

½ cup **orange juice**

2 tablespoons **mango syrup**

scant ½ cup **plum wine**

1 **pear**

Ingredients

⅔ cup **milk**

2⅔ cups **coconut cream**

4 **egg yolks**

½ cup **sugar**

4 teaspoons **white rum**

4 teaspoons **coconut liqueur**

2¼ cups **heavy cream**

1 **pineapple**

Coconut Ice Cream
with Pineapple

Preparation
SERVES 6

1 Heat the milk with the coconut cream in a pan. Beat the egg yolks in a heatproof bowl with the sugar until they are pale and fluffy, then stir in the milk mixture.

2 Place the bowl over a pan of barely simmering water and beat until thick, creamy, and light. Remove from the heat and stir in the rum and coconut liqueur. Whisk the cream until stiff, then carefully fold into the egg mixture.

3 Spoon the mixture into a flat, freezerproof container and place in the freezer for at least 2 hours, until set.

4 Peel, halve, and core the pineapple and cut the flesh into thin slices. Place them on serving plates. Divide the ice cream into wedges with a spoon, or if you like, use a scoop to form it into balls. Arrange on top of the pineapple slices and serve immediately.

Peach and Pear Raita
with Ginger

Feel like something sweet? In India, raitas are put on the table as refreshing side dishes, but this one also makes a brilliant dessert

Ingredients

2 peaches

2 pears

2 tablespoons sugar

juice of 1 lemon

2½ cups creamy plain yogurt

2 teaspoons grated fresh

ginger root

1 tablespoon honey

5 tablespoons heavy cream

¼ teaspoon ground ginger

Preparation
SERVES 4

1 Places the peaches in a bowl and pour in hot water to cover. Let stand for 2 minutes, then drain. Peel, halve, and pit the peaches, then dice the flesh. Peel the pears, cut into fourths, core, and dice the flesh.

2 Mix the peaches and pears with the sugar and 2 tablespoons of the lemon juice in a bowl, then let steep.

3 Combine the yogurt, the remaining lemon juice, the grated ginger, honey, and cream. Set aside a few pieces of fruit for decoration, then fold the remainder into the yogurt mixture. Serve sprinkled with the ground ginger and decorated with the reserved fruit.

This raita is also unforgettably delicious when made with mangoes and lychees. Alternatively, you can try it in the traditional way—as a cooling accompaniment to an Asian lentil dish.

Fruit Salad
in Pineapple Shells

Preparation
SERVES 4

1 Leaving the green leaves intact, cut the pineapples in half lengthwise, cut out and discard the cores, then remove the flesh from the skins with a small sharp knife. Cut the flesh into pieces and place in a bowl. Reserve the pineapple shells.

2 Peel the bananas and slice thinly. Peel the mango, cut the flesh away from the pit, and dice coarsely. Peel, halve, and pit the rambutans or lychees. Place all the fruit in a bowl and mix together.

3 Heat the palm sugar with 1 tablespoon water, stirring until it has dissolved. Remove from the heat, stir in the lime juice, and let cool slightly. Pour the sugar solution over the fruit and stir gently. Spoon the fruit salad into the pineapple halves and place on dessert plates.

4 Peel and slice the kiwi fruits. Peel off the physalis husks, and wash the fruits. Garnish the plates with kiwi fruit slices and physalis. If you like, serve the fruit salad sprinkled with pieces of lime rind.

Ingredients

2 small **pineapples**

2 small **bananas**

½ ripe **mango**

4 **rambutans** (or lychees)

2 heaping tablespoons **palm sugar**

1 tablespoon **lime juice**

2 **kiwi fruits** · 8 **physalis**

Ingredients

¼ cup **palm sugar** · 3 **eggs**

1½ cups **coconut milk**

pinch of freshly grated **nutmeg**

pinch of **ground allspice**

pinch of **ground cardamom**

2 tablespoons **pistachio nuts**

oil, for brushing

confectioners' sugar and ground

cinnamon, for dusting

Coconut Custards
with Pistachios

Preparation
SERVES 4

1 Dissolve the palm sugar in 2 tablespoons hot water. Whisk the eggs in a bowl and stir in the dissolved sugar. Add the coconut milk, nutmeg, allspice, and cardamom.

2 Preheat the oven to 400°F. Pour water to a depth of 1–1½ inches into a roasting pan and heat in the oven.

3 Coarsely chop the pistachios. Brush four ramekins with oil. Divide the pistachios among them, then spoon in the

coconut custard. Cover with foil, place in the roasting pan, and bake for 1 hour.

4 Remove the ramekins from the oven, let cool, then chill in the refrigerator for 3 hours. Loosen the custards around the edge with the blade of a knife and invert onto dessert plates. Before serving, decorate, if you like, with fresh coconut and dust with confectioners' sugar and ground cinnamon.

Green Tea Sherbet
with Mint and Rum

One last treat that nobody wants to miss: A sherbet is always welcome, especially when it has such fragrant aromas of green tea and mint

Ingredients

½ white gelatin leaf

⅔ cup sugar

¾ cup green tea leaves

1 cup fresh mint leaves

scant ½ cup glucose

½ cup lemon juice

scant ½ cup light cream

2 tablespoons white rum

Preparation
SERVES 4

1 Soak the gelatin in a small bowl of cold water. Pour 2¼ cups water into a small pan, add the sugar, and bring to a boil. Remove from the heat and stir in the tea leaves, mint leaves, and glucose.

2 Cover the pan and let steep for 8–10 minutes, then strain through a fine strainer. Squeeze out the gelatin, stir it into the liquid with the lemon juice, then let cool.

3 Stir the cream and the rum into the cooled liquid. Pour the mixture into a flat, freezerproof dish and place in the freezer for 30 minutes, or until ice crystals began to form around the edges. Tip the sherbet into a bowl and beat vigorously with a fork to break up the ice crystals. Return the sherbet to the container and re-freeze. Beat the sherbet two or three more times.

4 Before serving, form the sherbet into balls with a spoon or scoop. If you like, arrange in bowls on a bed of stirred sherbet.

Sherbets are undisputed winners as desserts. You can also offer a sherbet as a refresher between two courses. It cleanses the taste buds, and helps to settle the stomach.

Index of Recipes

© Verlag Zabert Sandmann, Munich

Graphic design: Georg Feigl, Barbara Markwitz
Recipes: ZS team
Editors: Gertrud Köhn, Kathrin Ullerich, Angelika Schulz
Production: Karin Mayer, Peter Karg-Cordes
Lithography: inteca Media Service Ltd., Rosenheim
Printing & Binding: Officine Grafiche De Agostini, Novara

English translation: Translate-A-Book, Oxford UK
Typesetting: Organ Graphic, Abingdon, UK
Editing: Linda Doeser Publishing Services, London, UK

This edition published by Barnes & Noble, Inc.,
by arrangement with Zabert Sandmann.
2002 Barnes & Noble Books
M 11 10 9 8 7 6 5 4 3 2 1
Printed in Italy
ISBN: 0-7607-3722-3

Visit us also at our Internet website at **www.zsverlag.de**

Photo Credits

Cover photos: Stockfood/Harry Bischof (front cover); Stockfood/Stan Irvine (back cover right); Stockfood/S. & P. Eising (back cover center); Stockfood/D. Loftus (back cover left)

Walter Cimbal: 9 (above center), 64; Susie Eising: 15, 55, 73, 82–83, 92, 93; Jo Kirchherr: 8, 9 (below), 30, 31, 39; Stockfood/Bayside: 70, 75; Stockfood/Harry Bischof: 37; Stockfood/Michael Boyny: 63; Stockfood/Gerhard Bumann: 7 (below center); Stockfood/Jean Cazals: 67, 71, 85: Stockfood/Cephas, Tim Hill: 87; Stockfood/Thom DeSanto; 4–5; Stockfood/Eising (M): 21; Stockfood/Susie Eising: 10–11, 16, 17, 24, 25, 41, 46, 47, 52, 53, 89, Stockfood/S. & P. Eising: 2–3, 7 (above left, second from below left, below left, above right), 13, 19, 27, 29, 33, 34–35, 51, 59, 61, 69, 81, 88; Stockfood/Wieder Frank: 43, 77; Stockfood/Ulrike Köb: 91; Stockfood/Sian Irvine: 23; Stockfood: Nicolas Leser: 49; Stockfood/D. Loftus: 56–57, 79; Stockfood/Joris Luyten: 76; Stockfood: Karl Newedel: 6 (right); Stockfood/W. Reavell: 40, 65; Stockfood/Rosenfeld Images Ltd.: 6 (left); Stockfood/Snowflake Studios Inc.: 45; Stockfood/Maximilian Stock Ltd.: 7 (second from above left); Stockfood/Bernhard Winkelmann: 95